C++: L
Like a Boss

A Beginners Guide in Coding Programming And Dominating C++. Novice to Expert Guide To Learn and Master C++ Fast

By: Isaac D. Cody

© **Copyright 2014 by Isaac D. Cody- All rights reserved.**

This document is geared towards providing exact and reliable information in regards to the topic and issue covered. The publication is sold with the idea that the publisher is not required to render accounting, officially permitted, or otherwise, qualified services. If advice is necessary, legal or professional, a practiced individual in the profession should be ordered.

- From a Declaration of Principles which was accepted and approved equally by a Committee of the American Bar Association and a Committee of Publishers and Associations.

In no way is it legal to reproduce, duplicate, or transmit any part of this document in either electronic means or in printed format. Recording of this publication is strictly prohibited and any storage of this document is not allowed unless with written permission from the publisher. All rights reserved.

The information provided herein is stated to be truthful and consistent, in that any liability, in terms of inattention or otherwise, by any usage or abuse of any policies, processes, or directions contained within is the solitary and utter responsibility of the recipient reader. Under no circumstances will any legal responsibility or blame be held against the publisher for any reparation, damages, or monetary loss due to the information herein, either directly or indirectly.

Respective authors own all copyrights not held by the publisher.

The information herein is offered for informational purposes solely, and is universal as so. The presentation of the information is without contract or any type of guarantee assurance.

The trademarks that are used are without any consent, and the publication of the trademark is without permission or backing by the trademark owner. All trademarks and brands within this book are for clarifying purposes only and are the owned by the owners themselves, not affiliated with this document.

Table of Contents

Chapter 1: Basic Background, History, and the Fruition of C++

Chapter 2: Let's Begin

Chapter 3: Diving more into Program Comments, Data Types, Lines, and Characters

Chapter 4: Arrays, Loops, and Conditions

Chapter 5: Working with Operators

Chapter 6: Constants and the various types of Literals

Conclusion

Bonus: Brief Hacking History and Overview

Chapter 1: Basic Background, History, and the Fruition of C++

Before we get into how to start using C++, you have to learn what it is, and how it came about. The reason for this is simple. To truly know something, you have to know everything you possibly can learn about the subject, especially when it comes to something so technical such as computer programming.

C++ is a very important part of computer and Internet history. It is simply something that is interwoven within the history of the technological world, as we know today. Furthermore, the apps and other functions on a smart phone would not exist if it were not for C++.

When you are learning C++, you will be filled with wonder at the fact that one programming language can have so much impact in our daily lives. Almost every computer ever built can be attributed to a specific aspect that can be traced back to the language of C++. One of the benefits of learning this language is the ability to learn other languages with ease. Having the ability of learning C++ will enhance your knowledge of other programming language, which is why many people regard it as the 'godfather' of computer programming. Furthermore, many big companies still need programmers that have C++ as they rely this programming language to run their central computer system. So when the going gets tough, just know it'll benefit you in the long run so stay strong and get in the programming mindset!

History of C++

Bjarne Strousup was working on his thesis for his doctorate, and he decided to work with a programming language that was known as Simula. This language one one of the first programming languages of the computer age. However it was very slow and full of bugs.

Strousup came up with the idea of C with Classes. A programming language that was a lot faster than Simula. C with classes later became Cfront which sped up the process of creating a language. However, Cfront was left in the dust when C++ came along, because it added compilers into the language, making it a lot easier, and faster to use than any other project language of the time.

Since then there have been annotated reference guides and updates to the language to make it better and faster, and even easier to use. C++ for Dummies is a popular guide for this language.

C++ is one of the most popular languages out there today. This language is the best for many industries, so rather than make a new language which takes a lot of time, they just adapt C++ to many different variations because it is versatile in its nature.

Exactly what is C++

C++ is not just any programming language, it is object oriented. Object oriented programming or OOP for short, is programming that revolves around objects rather than actions. It is like looking at the whole picture at once, rather than each individual puzzle piece.

This programming language was designed with flexibility and speed in mind, as other languages of the time were way too slow, and could only do one thing, so every time you wanted to create something new, you needed a new language.

There are many things that you can use this language for, and they are still very much popular today, despite the ominous amount of languages that are out there now.

- Prepackaged scripts: These are what script enthusiasts, and new hackers use to practice their programming techniques. Since so many people nowadays want to take the easy way out, scripts that come already prepared are what most hackers are looking for, thus the packages need to improve, and they do so using C++.

- Video Games: Let's face it, pretty much everyone plays video games at some point in their life. Whether it is growing up, or when you have kids, you will get sucked into the realm of video games, and you can never escape. Those games can be attributed to some way or form from using the C++ language. If you are into making games, and bringing the world joy through graphics, then it is definitely a good idea to learn the language of C++

- Web pages: A lot of web pages are made using C++. The reason for this is because the language is so easy to manipulate, it makes for a quick and easy website that has plenty of interactive features for people. Some websites you may visit often that are created with C++ are Amazon and Ebay. If you like designing web pages you should learn C++ to be efficient and maybe even land a decent job in this field.

- Phone Apps: Nowadays it seems everyone has a smart phone, and that means apps galore. There are thousands of apps out there, and more are being made every day. Some apps are free, some apps cost money, but a good chunk were made using C++. That is because this language is so scalable that it can be used for simple games and more intricate shopping apps.

There are a lot of other minor things that C++ is used for, such as VoIP calling. That was created using C++. The fact of the matter is, you will get told time and time again that C++ is a dying language when in reality that is just a ruse that JAVA people uses to scare people into switching languages to ensure that C++ is a dying language.

Why It's used

C++ is used not only for its flexibility and speed, but because it has a lot of components, it is fairly easy to learn, and if you master C++, you can master the other languages with ease. The reason for this is that when you learn something that is a little more complex than everything else first, the easier stuff will fall right into place, however, if you get used to easy to learn subjects, then you will find that the more difficult stuff is hard to learn because you are not used to putting in that much effort into the subject that you are trying to learn.

If you want to learn a language that you can use for different types of functions within the realm of computer technology, then this is the language for you. You can do almost anything with it, and once you learn enough about it, you may be able to figure out ways to manipulate the language to do things that it generally cannot do.

C++ is a very important language when it comes to computer programming, and though it has a lot of variables from the way that it is laid out, it is very easy to read, and very easy to create. This makes it one of the most desired programming languages that are out there, because no one wants to struggle to read code. No one wants to have to spend all of their time out there working on what they know is right just because they cannot find where they went wrong.

Job Outlook

Yes, there are a lot of jobs out there that still rely on C++ to operate. There are so many different things that you could do, and all of them affect other people in the community. Video game designing, and web page designing are two of the most prominent things that are out there. You could also become a white hat or blue hat hacker.

But according to payscale.com (search software engineer), a person with C++ Software engineer background can earn up to $57,000 to $120,000 based on experience. The median is around $80,363. Some other titles that people with C++ programming language have is Computer Programmer, Electrical Engineer, and Application Developer.

However, to be the best that you can be, you should always know two or three programming languages to be marketable. Though those languages will not be included in this book, do not marry yourself to a single language. Instead, just like with human language, broaden your horizons and dabble in a few, but keep one as your main language.

C++ should be the main language that you fall back on due to its versatility. Maybe use JAVA or Linux as your other languages, but C++ is the best main language to have, and you only want the best as your main.

C++ is a statically written lower level language which means that it is a clean cut expansive language.

C++ is a fully functional super set of C that supports object oriented programming. This means that it supports all the pillars of OOP, such as encapsulation, data hiding, inheritance and polymorphism.

To learn more about object oriented programming, you can do a quick search online, and find out more about it. It is best to get some knowledge about what it is, but it is not quintessential to your knowledge of C++, so it will not really be included in this book, except for a few mentions in passing, and some tidbits of information here and there.

Three Important Components of C++

The standard C++ is made up of three very important concepts.

- Core Language: This is made up of all the variables, data types, literals, and other important aspects of the language, creating building blocks to get to the next level

- C++ Standard Library: this allows you to manipulate files, and other workings within the language, and bend them to your will.

- STL: This stands for Standard Template Library, which gives you functions to manipulate data structures and variables and other things of the sort.

Why is C++ considered the best language out there?

Well, aside from the copiously mentioned flexibility, speed, and simplicity, it is a language that has spanned over thirty years, and is still widely used today. There are not many products in any genre of life out there that can say the same. Products and companies come and go, but only true perfection stays. Well that is how the saying goes. To be honest, C++ has had many updates since then, but the core process is still the same. When it came out it was light years ahead of its time, and today it is still a pretty advanced piece of technology, due to the updates that keep it on top.

There are a lot of opinions that also have to do with why C++ is considered the best. While there are a lot of people who say that C++ is no longer relevant, even more vouch that it is still the best language out there, and it is their fall back language. It is the one they know the most about, and the one they carry close to their heart. The reasons vary, but the fact that 90% of programmers default to C++ shows that it is very much the best programming language out there today.

C++ is one of the few languages that follow the ANSI standard completely, which is why some of the best games you will ever play are still written with C++. Because their compilers are set to ensure that all commands are written and executed without errors. It can also be used across many different types of platforms, whether you have a Microsoft, Unix, Mac, Windows, or and Alpha device, it is possible to use C++. This is a great thing, because a lot of programmers have to operate across many different platforms, and the universality makes it easy and portable. Just throw your code on a flash drive and upload it wherever it is needed.

Benefits of using the C++ language

There are a lot of benefits that you will be able to enjoy when using the C++ language. Some of these benefits include:

- The big library: since C++ has been around for along time, they have a library that is pretty large. This is available for you to use so you can pick out the codes that you want inside of your script and save some time and even learn some new things. You can also create some of your own codes if you wish, but this library can be really helpful for the beginner who is learning and can make it easier than ever to get the code written.

- Ability to work with other languages: C++ is a great language to use with some of the other programming languages out there. This makes it easier to really work on the projects that you want because you can add in the parts that you like from different coding languages and combine them together to get something really amazing.

- Works on many projects: most other programming languages are going to focus on just one or two little projects. For example, using JavaScript means that you are just going to be working on websites. But with C++, you are able to use it to help with a lot of different projects. Whether you are looking to work on a website, looking to create a new program, or do something else with programming, you will be able to do it with the help of C++.

- Fast and reliable: if you have used some of the other coding languages that are popular in the past, you will find that sometimes they aren't the most reliable. Information may slip through or they won't start working the way that you would like. If you want something that works the first time and is reliable, then it is a good idea to go with C++.

- Offers a lot of power: those who like to work in programming and want to have a lot of power in the work that they are doing will find that C++ is the right option for them to choose. It has some of the best power for the programming languages that are out there.

These are just a few of the benefit that you can enjoy when you are using the C++ programming language. It may seem a bit more difficult to use than some of the others, such as Python, but it has a lot of the power that you need and can work well with other programming languages. With a bit of practice, you are going to get all the basics of this language down and really enjoy what you are able to do with this programming language.

Chapter 2: Let's Begin

Let's begin! There are a lot of places we can start, but let's talk about environments first. While you do not really need to set up your own environment, as there are many online. An environment is a compiler of your choice that takes your code, and does all of the functions for you. In the old days, you would have to open your command prompts and create an environment to use, but those days are over. A simple mistake back in the day could do some serious damage to their computers. Now you can practice some risky prompts without any risk to your device whatsoever.

There are many examples to try out and use on the internet. To try them out, the easiest place to go is http://www.compileonline.com Choose the "Learn C++" option down at the bottom, and it will take you to where you need to go.

Here is an example to try. The output should be the words "**Try This**".

```
#include <iostream>

using namespace std;

int main ()
{
        court << "Use This One!";
        return 0;
}
```

Now you can choose to type these codes into the compiler directly, or you can write several, and save them to your computer, and access them whenever, so that you don't have to retype them every time you want to mess with them. You can use several different types of text editors. However, some of them are device type specific. This means they only work on the type of device that you create them on.

The text editors that you can use are OS edit command, Brief, EMACS, epsilon, Windows Notepad, vlm or vl. However, only vlm and vl are multi platform usable. Make sure to save the files with the extension .c or .cpp.

You should start in a text editor to get the rough draft going on your program before you even think of moving to a compiler. This is because once you get to a compiler, it is a lot easier to mess up on your program, and not catch it. However, if you have it laid out in a nice, clean-cut fashion in a text editor, then you should have no problems with getting things going in the compiler.

C++ Compilers

There are many different compilers out there, and a lot of them are pretty expensive. Those compilers are for the elite programmers who have mastered the lower level compilers already. Beginners only need a basic compiler, and most of those are free. However, just like with anything that is free, you have to be careful of what you are getting. There are more bad cheap compliers than good ones out there so on the pretense of being free, I would suggest you paying additional functions past the start up page. These additional functions are usually very cheap anyways so you won't have to break the bank to get them.

One of the most popular compilers available is the GNU C/C++ compiler. It is used most commonly in UNIX and Linux installations. To see if you already have the compiler, pull up the command line in your UNIX/Linux application and type in the following

$ g++ -v

If the compiler is installed, then you should see this message on the screen:

Using built-in specs.

Target: i386-redhat-linux

Configured with: ../configure –prefix=/usr ......

Thread model: posix

gcc version 4.1.2 20080704 (Red Hat 4.1.2-46)

If this message does not come up on your screen, the compiler either isn't on the computer or you installed it incorrectly and you will need to go through and get it properly installed.

In this book, we will go over how to install using the Windows platform. If you have a different platform, then you should go to http://gcc.gnu.org/install/ and read the instructions on how to download it onto your platform.

To install this compiler on your Windows computer, you will need to first install MinGW. This is the software that makes the compiler compatible with your computer, and it is very important that you have this software, otherwise you will not even be able to download the compiler at all.

To install this software, you can go to the homepage of the software at www.mingw.org and allow it to direct you to where you need to go. Once you install that you should install gcc core, gcc-g++, MinGW runtime and blnutlls, at the bare minimum, but you can install more if you would like. Once you are done with the install, you can run all of the GNU tools from the Command line on Windows.

Now that you have everything set up to where you can run it, you can start learning more about how to run the programs themselves.

Basic Syntax

C++ can be defined as not only the program, but objects that collectively communicate by invoking other methods. When you are working with C++ you should know what four things mean above all else.

Class- This is a template or a blueprint that states the object and its support type, and describes the behaviors of an object. This means that objects are sorted by their behaviors and their actions/supports into classes that fit the description of the object in question.

Object- Objects have behaviors and states. For example, if you look at a dog, it has states. These states could be classified as color, breed, name, standard of breed (AKC/AKA/APC registries). "Dogs" also show certain behaviors as well. They wag their tails, they bark, they pant, they eat dry kibble, and they go to the bathroom outside in the yard. These things make dogs a *unique object*. These objects are classified into groups know as, you guessed it, classes.

Method- This is another term for behavior. There can be as many or as few as you choose in your classes. This is where all of the data is manipulated, and actions are played out, along with the place that all of the logic is written. Methods are especially important because without them, your program would not know what it is supposed to do with the variable that you give it. It would just sit there like a dud and do nothing.

Instant Variables- These refer to each individual object. Each object is classified with a unique set of these variables that act as a fingerprint for an object. These variables are assigned to the object by using values that occur whenever the object is created.

Now that you know the four main definitions of programming, Let's take a look at a code that you can write that will print out: **"Try This"**. Unlike the example above, this will explain a little more in depth what you are wanting to do, and the reason for each function.

#include <iostream>

using namespace std;

// main() [this is when the program will begin to execute.]

int main()
{

cout << "Try This"; // [Prints Try This]

return 0;

}

This function will allow you to print whatever you want, not just the words "Try This".

Now let's break down the various aspects of the program that is set out above. There are several different aspects of this language that you have to take in consideration. Each aspect is important in getting it to run, and if you do not execute them entirely.

Headers- There are several headers out there for C++, and all of them are necessary or at the very least useful to your programming operations. However, for most functions you will see the header that is above <iostream>. When you use a header be sure to enclose it properly, and put **#include before** it to prompt the program to use that header.

Namespace- Namespaces are a fairly new addition to C++, only coming about in the 2011 update. They do not do much, other than describe which namespace to use. While they are not necessary, they save you a lot of confusion on functions of a program. It simply act as a way to organize your functions more systematically.

Main- Here is where the main function begins. Using the line **// main()** instructs the program to start executing the main function of the program, and start the out put process. It is essential that you set up the main function command, otherwise your program will not know what it is supposed to be running, nor will it know when it is supposed to run. This will be seen as a single line comment inside the program and it is going to tell the program that the main function is beginning.

INT main- This is where the function execution officially begins. If you do not include this, the entire process will stop, because you did not introduce the variables, and without the variables, the program is lost.

Cout- This instructs the program to display the message that you want on the screen. If you do not put cout, chances are your program will may or may not fail. The problem is you don't know if you succeed or not so if you want to make sure that everything runs smoothly, be sure to add cout.

Return- This returns the value back to zero, and terminates the function. It instructs the program to end the process, and go back to the beginning.

Now to compile and execute your first official C++ program.

First you must know how to *save* the file. Open your chosen text editor, and enter the code that is seen above. Once you have done that, hit save as, and choose a file location that is easily found. For organization purposes, it is always best to have a separate folder for all of your programs. Save the file as hello.cpp, and once you have saved it, you should open up your command prompt before heading to the directory where the file is saved.

To get the file to open inside your compiler, start by typing 'g++ hello.cpp'. you can then press enter and the code will be opened properly. As long as there aren't any errors, the prompt is going to generate an a.out executable file. To run the program, type out 'o.out' and see the compiler work. The information that you should get on the compiler from this on the computer includes:

$ g++ hello.cpp

$ ./a.out

Try This

Make sure that you are inputting all of the variables the proper way, and remember, these things are case sensitive. If you do not input the functions the right way, you will find that things tend to go awry. The thing with coding is you have to be precise. This detailed oriented personal attributed applies to all programming languages! However, anyone can do it if they are willing to pay attention.

The basic function commands are not the only things that you need to use. There are other things that are important when you are building a prompt as well, as they too instruct the program to do specific things. Some of these things are blocks and semicolons.

You probably think a pause in a sentence when you think semicolon, however, they are complete stops in C++ programs. The semicolon indicates the termination of a statement. This means that each individual statement must be indicated by the use of a semicolon. The following are three different statements.

x=y;

y=y+1;

add(x,y);

Each one of those statements were separated by not only a line break, but also a semicolon. You could also do it this way.

x=y; y=y+1; add(x,y);

Each one of those will be recognized as separate statements simply because of the semicolon. It is kind of mind blowing how something so simple can have so much of an impact.

In this coding language, a block is going to be a set of statements that you enclose with brackets. These statements are logical entities that the program puts on the screen due to the main command prompt. For example

{

    cout << "I like Pizza">>; //prints I like Pizza

    return 0

}

The end of a line is not a terminator, as was indicated above. The semicolon is the only thing that terminates the statement.

Identifiers

Now let us move on to the identifiers in the program. These identifiers are used to identify multiple things, such as classes, modules, functions and variables within a block. An identifier is going to be a group of letters and numbers that you are able to name your program or your files and they must start with a letter, but can have any letter or number you want afterwards. There are no punctuation characters other than what you might see in a sentence that are allowed as identifiers. You will not see characters such as @,&,% or $, and the programming is case sensitive. That means YokoOno is different than Yokoono, yokoOno, and yokoono. Make sure that you are capitalizing only the letters that you should be capitalizing in your programs.

Though pretty much anything can be an identifier, there are some things that are reserved for keywords in C++, and can't be used as identifiers. These words are as follows.

asm		
Break	Bool	Auto
Char	Catch	Case
Const cast	Const	Class
Delete	Default	Continue
Dynamic cast	Double	Do
Explicit	Enum	Else
False	Extern	Export
Friend	For	Float
Inline	If	Goto
Mutable	Long	Int
Protected	Private	Namespace
Reinterpret cast	Register	Public
Signed	Short	Return
Static cast	Static	Sizeof
Template	Switch	Struct
True	Throw	This
Typeid	Typedef	Try
Unsigned	Unlon	Typename

Void	Virtual	Using
While	Wchar t	Volatile

Everything else is fair game when it comes to identifiers. Think of identifiers as usernames and passwords. Mix it up, but make sure that they are functional.

Trigraphs

Trigraphs are going to be sequences of three characters that will represent just one character. You will notice these because they are going to start out with two questions marks at the beginning. Seems a little redundant to use three characters when one will work, but the reason behind this is so you do not confuse the program with the meaning of the character, as many are similar.

Here are some frequently used trigraphs to give you an example of what we mean.

??=	#
??/	\
??'	^
??(	[
??)	]
??!	|
??<	{
??>	}
??-	~

Not all compilers support trigraphs due to their confusing nature, and most people try to stay away from them, however, it has been found that when you memorize trigraphs, you are less likely to mess up by hitting the wrong symbol in your function.

Whitespace

Moving on to whitespace. This is the empty lines in a program. Sometimes they contain comments, and these are known as blank lines. The compilers completely ignore them. Whitespace describes blanks, new lines, tabs, characters and comments. It is merely used to make your program look more organized and readable.

There should be at least one line of whitespace between the variable/identifier and the statement.

QUIZ

You thought that you could just waltz through this book without being tested on if you were paying attention? No cheating either! Just because you can peek at the answers does not mean that you should. You should take it just like a normal quiz to truly test your knowledge so you can figure out if you need to go back and re-read over some things. This is a short quiz, so you will be okay.

1. What is whitespace?

2. Fill in the blanks ____ <<x=y+1_>>

3. What are trigraphs?

4. Who Invented the C with Classes language?

5. What is the header used in most functions?

Answers

1. The blank spaces or comments that the compiler ignores

2. Cout <<x=y+1;>>

3. A sequence of three characters that represent a single character

4. Bjarne Strousup

5. <iostream>

Congratulations, if you got all five right, then you can move on to the next section! However, if you got more than one wrong, then you should probably go back and reread the section. If you're ready then onwards to Chapter 3.

Chapter 3: Diving more into Program Comments, Data Types, Lines, and Characters

Now that we have covered the bare basics of C++ it is time to get into some more in depth subjects that surround the program. While these are more in depth, they are still a paramount concepts all beginners need to learn.

Program Comments

So, there are going to be times when you will want to write some comments inside of your code. These are important because they allow you to leave a little message inside the code so that others who are reading through it later on will be able to get a good look at exactly how your code is ran and also provide "referral" to what you're trying to accomplish in your code. Furthermore, leaving notes within the lines of your code is a good way to notify yourself where a code might have gone wrong. By putting comments inside your codes, you are more likely to know where you succeed or where you went wrong.

These comments can be as simple or as complex as you would like. Some people will just place in one or two words if that is all that is needed to help out the other users, but there are other times when you are going to need to combine a few more lines into the mix to ensure that it is all going to work out and that the other person understands what is going on inside of the code.

In this language, you will just need to use the // symbol in order to show that you are writing out a comment. You can make it as long as you would like, just make sure that when the comment is done, you skip to the next line so that the program knows that it is supposed to start reading through it again.

The program is going to stop reading after the // and it is not going to affect the way that the program works. Other programmers who look at the code will see the comments that you write, but when the program is executed, these comments are going to be skipped. You can add in as many as you would like to your program, but do try to keep them a bit limited because it can start to clog up the code and make it hard to read and understand.

Program comments are basically the statements that are inside the code. The statements, or comments, are going to be there to help others who use your code understand what the purpose of each function is. All program languages allow for some type of comments, but they do not allow all of the kinds of comments that are out there. The most common to use is a single line comment. This is what all program languages allow for. These comments are simple explanatory lines that tell the next reader what the purpose is in a simple sentence.

There are also multiple line comments. This is one that very few program languages allow for. C++ is one of those few languages. Sometimes you have a more complex explanation, and it needs to span over more than one line. This is possible to do in C++.

When you are using a single line comment, you will see that it is written out in the code with // and can go all the way to the end of your line. An example of this is:

{

    cout << "that's great" >>; //prints that's great

    return 0

}

will have the final output of "that's great" and nothing else. The comment is ignored by the compiler so that you can let other programmers in on what the code is for, or what you need done to the code.

However if you are trying to get some help on a code, you should use a multi line comment so that you can easily get the best out of your complicated code. Multi line comments are surrounded by these symbols /*-*/. Typed out like that it almost looks like an emoji. For example

/* I need help making the puppet dance*/ is a comment. However, that is still a single line comment still. A better example would be

/* I need help making the puppet dance

*All he does at this point is sway from side to side */

That would be a multi line comment. As you can see, when you start a new line you should put the asterisk at the beginning to indicate to the program that you are still writing a comment and that the next line is indeed whitespace. When compiled it will ignore the comments and only show what you want it to show.

While you can mix the comment styles, it is best to keep them separated for now, until you get the hang of everything.

Data Types

You have to use different variables when you are writing a program using any language. These are nothing more than just reserved memory values that store locations in some space in the memory of the compiler. The above list of reserved keywords are useful here as well. While there are a lot of keywords, there are seven basic keywords that define data types.

Type	Keyword
Wide character	Wchar_t
Valueless	Void
Double floating point	Double
Floating point	Float
Integer	Int
Character	Char
Boolean	bool

Most of the data types that you can use can be modified using one of these following modifiers to help:

Long,

Short

Unsigned

Signed

Variable Types Cont...

When you are using variables inside of a coding language, you are providing some storage space that makes it easier to for the program to manipulate. All of the variables that you use will be attached to a different type and these types are going to determine the layout and the size of the memory of the variable. It is also going to set a range of values that you are able to store on this memory space.

Naming the variable is going to be similar to naming the identifier. You will only be able to name it with a letter or an underscore and the letters are going to be case sensitive. But after that, you are able to use any type of digit, letter, and character that you would like.

Again, the basic variables that you will be able to use here in more detail include:

- Wchart_t: this is the wide character type.
- Void: this is going to represent the absence of a type
- Double: this is a floating value that will have double precision.
- Float: this is a floating point that is going to have single precision.
- Int: this is an integer
- Char: this is often going to be just one byte and is a type of integer.
- Bool: this is going to work with values that are either true or false.

You can also define other types of variables. These variables are things line pointer, array, reference, enumeration, data structures, and classes.

Creating a new line

Now that you know the data types and modifiers, and all about making a comment in your program, it is time to learn about how to create a new line. This is a problem that a lot of new programmers run into. They have their program all nice and laid out in the input, but the output is still really mashed together and really unkempt. This is because they did not properly create a new line. Remember that whitespace is ignored, so you cannot just skip a line, and expect to have a line skipped in your program. You have to indicate to the compiler that you want to start a new line. This is really important, as when you play out your program, you want it to run smoothly. You do not want to see something like this.

Try This Today I ate Pizza and I did math. 6= (7-1) that what I learned today.

You would probably rather see this.

Try This

today I ate pizza and I did math

6=(7-1)

that is what I learned today

To make the distinction, you have to have the right function, as that is what programming relies on, having the correct function.

To create a line break, you have to use the function endl; this will indicate that you want a line break, and you do not even have to add whitespace if you do not want to, though it is recommended because it makes your program easier to read for a human.

For example, this:

```
{
        cout << Try This;>> endl;

        <<Today I ate Pizza and did Math;>> endl;

        <<6=(7-1);>> endl;

        << That is what I learned today;>> endl;

        return 0
}
```

Looks way better than this:

```
{
        cout << Try This;>> endl; << Today I ate Pizza and did Math;>> endl; <<6=(7-1);>> endl; << That is what I learned today;>> endl;

        return 0
}
```

Can you see how confusing that would get for someone reading the code? You want your code file to be easy to read, so that if someone else has to fix something, they can easily find where the mistake has been made. If everything is all jumbled together, then they would not be able to find anything very easily, now would they?

You can also indicate line breaks by using /n This is the same thing as endl; but is a lot faster to type. You can use whichever method you want but choose one and stick with it.

The importance of the basics of C++

I know what you are thinking, why must you know all these nonsense tidbits of information when you are just beginning, and the reason is, if you don't learn them now, you won't think that you will need them in the future, and then when you are reading a program that someone else wrote, you will be wondering what all of those extra characters mean, and why there is so much whitespace. Creating a habit of these simple yet somewhat tedious tasks is paramount if mastering more complicated programming methods. Just like mastering any sort of language, you have to master the basics to master the expert level concepts.

Variable definitions

A variable definitions instructs the compiler how much and where to store and create the variable. It specifies the data type and lists one or more of the variables of the type. For example

type variable_list;

You have to have a valid data type that is listed above. They may contain one or more identifier names as long as they are separated by commas, such as

int ---- j,k,l;

char----c,ch;

float---- f, salary;

double--- d;

Each of these abbreviations instructs the compiler to create variables of that type with those names. Variables can be assigned with an initial value, by indicating such with an equal sign. For example

#include <iostream>

using namespace std;

int. main ()

int j=10;

int k=5;

int l=j+k

{

    cout <<l>> endl;

    return 0

}

You should get the answer 15

You can also declare and define the variables in your program, but that is some higher level stuff, so if you would like to look into it you can google search a tutorial on that.

QUIZ

Here is the set up. You should have one phrase, a math problem, and then the answer to the math problem using said integers. You can make up all of the variables yourself, whatever you want them to be.

#using <header>

using namespace std;

int main ()

int _=_

int _=_

int _=_+_

{

    cout < "";> /n

    < "";> /n

    cout < "int_";> /n

    return 0

}

Simply enter your digits in and make sure your numbers add up. After you've done so, rerun the code without relying on copying and pasting the code without the intergers. This way, you'll have a basic understanding of variables and playing with the basic integers operations within C++.

Chapter 4: Arrays, Loops, and Conditions

Believe it or not, you've learned so much already. The basics are really not that hard and now it's just about learning about a few more things and putting concept after concept together to make sure you're becoming a better C++ programmer. Let's keep going.

Arrays

Arrays are a data structure in C++ that will be able to store elements that are basically the same type and also a fixed size. Basically a collection of same type variables. Instead of using the individual variables, you would declare one array of variables such as numbers. To do this you use the numbers 0 to 99 and access each one by an index of the array.

Arrays are going to be memory locations that are continuous. The lowest is always the first element and then the highest element is going to be the last.

Initializing arrays

You can initialize arrays one by one or using a single statement. Example

double balance [5]= {1000.0, 2.0, 3.4, 17.0, 50.0};

The numbers that are found between the bracket can't end up higher than the amount of elements that you are using. This means that you cannot have six sets of numbers when your array title only specified five. However, if you do not specify the size, then an array of just the right size is created. You would type it as follows double balance [] {1000.0, 2.0, 3.4, 17.0, 50.0};

This creates the exact same array as the previous example, only you did not specify the array size so it was created for you. Pretty nifty.

Now that you know how to write an array, it is time to move on to putting it into the actual program. This program is a bit more advanced than the ones before, and has a few more elements. You can look up these elements on www.compileonline.com. You will be directed to a lot of tutorials and there is even a PDF file for you to download.

Here is the formula for your program to assign an array.

#include <iostream>

```cpp
using namespace std;

#include <iomanip>
using std::setw;

int main ()
{
    int n[ 10 ];  //n is an array of ten integers
    // initialize elements of array n to 0
    for ( int i=0; I <10; i++)
    {
        n[i] =i+100; // set ekement at location I to i+ 100
    }
    cout << element << setw(13) << value<< endl:
    //output each array element's value
    for (int j=0; j<10; j++)
    {
        cout << setw(7)<< j << setw(13) <<n[j] << endl;
    }
```

return 0

}

This program was able to use the setw() function in order to format the output that you see.

Loop Types

The loop types are used any time that you would like to take one type of code and execute it over and over. These statements are going to be done one right after the other. The loop statement will make it easier to execute these statements as many times as you would like.

There are four types of loops. These loops handle different requirements.

While loop

The While loop is going to continue repeating the loop as long as a certain condition is met. It is going to test out this condition each time it restarts the loop cycle and will do this until the condition is no longer true.

Written like this

while (condition)
{
    statement(s);
}

For Loop

This loop executes a statement sequence over and over again while abbreviating the code that manages the loop variables.

Written like this

for (init; condition; increment)
{
    statement(s);
}

Do.. while loop

The Do...while loop is going to be similar to the while statement, but it is going to test the condition when you reach the end of your statement, rather than the beginning.

Written like this

```
do
    {
        statement(s);
}while (condition);
```

Nested loops

The nested loop is going to have a loop that works inside of another loop, to create a continuous loop of loops. This one can get confusing after awhile.

Written like this

```
while (condition)
{
    while (condition)
    {
        statement(s)
```

}

　　　statement(s) // you can put more statements

}

Why is this important

Eventually you are going to want to branch out. I would highly recommend to further enhance your C++knowledge of the basics to ensure mastery and better understanding of more difficult tasks.

Though these may seem like they are too advanced for some or too easy for others, it's always good to do other practices and tutorials to enrich your programming skills. You can find tutorials at www.compileonline.com. It cannot be stressed enough how much of an essential tool this is. You have to check it out for yourself, and find out just how useful it really is. There are tutorials for other languages as well, not just C++ dabble around and see what you like.

Chapter 5: Working with Operators in C++

With any of the coding languages that you plan to use, it is important that you learn how to use the operators. These are going to help you to tell the program what you would like to do and can make dealing with your own codes so much easier. There are four main types of operators that you are able to use inside your program and they will each tell the program how to behave in a different way. Some of the operators that you will be able to use with the C++ language include:

- Logical operators
- Arithmetic operators
- Assignment operators
- Relational operators

Let's take a look at how some of these work and how you can bring them out to work well when writing code in the C++ language.

Logical operators

The first type of operator that we are going to use in this guidebook are the logical operators. These are going to help you to compare some of the parts that you are putting into the system. Some of the logical operators that you can work with include:

• (||): this is known as the logical OR. With this one, the condition is going to be true if one of your operands is not zero.

• (&&): this one is known as the logical AND. If you have two operands and they are not zero, your condition is true.

• (!): this is the logical NOT. You will be able to use this to reverse the status of your operand. So if the condition ends up being false, this sign will make it true.

Arithmetic operators

Another of the operators that you are able to use is the arithmetic operators. These are pretty much the same as using math in school. You are going to tell the program to add, subtract, and do other equations with the information that you are providing. Some of the arithmetic operators that you are able to use include:

- (+): this is the addition operator that will add together two operands of your choices.

- (-): this is the subtraction operator. It is going to take the right hand operand and subtract it from the left hand operand.

- (*): this is the operator that makes it possible to do multiplication in the C++ language.

- (/): this operator helps you to do division in C++.

- (++): this is the increment operator. It is going to increase the value of your operand by one.

- (--): this is the decrement operator. It is going to decrease the operand value by just one.

Assignment operators

The assignment operators will make it easier for you to assign a name to your variable and can help with searching for, saving, and so on with the different parts of the code that you are writing. Some of the assignment operators that you may use inside of C++ include:

- (=): this operator is the simple assignment operator. It is going to assign the value of the operand on the right hand to the one that is on the left.

- (+): this one is called the Add AND operator. It is going to add together the values from both operands and then assigns the sum of these over to the operand on the left side.

- (*=): this is the Multiply AND operator. It is going to multiply both of the operands and then gives the results over to the operand on the left side.

- (-=): this is the one that will subtract the value of your operand on the right side from the one on the left and then gives this difference to the left operand.

- (/=): this is the divide and operator. It is going to divide the value that is on the left side from the one on the right side and then assigns this amount to the left side.

There are a few other assignment operators that are available, but they are more advanced so we will just stick with some of these basic ones to help keep things in order!

Relational Operators

Relational operators can be really helpful when you are working inside of the C++ language. Some of the ones that you can use include:

- (==): this is the operator that is going to check the equality of your two operands. If they are equal, the conditions will be true.

- (>): this operator is going to check the value of your operands. If the operand on the left side is higher than the one on the right, the condition will be true.

- (<): this operator is basically the opposite of the one above. If you find that the value of your operand on the left side is greater than the one on the right side, the condition will be true.

- (!=): this one is going to check the equality of your two operands and if the values are unequal, your condition is true.

- (<=): this operator is going to check whether the operand on the left side is less than or equal to the operand on the right side. If it meets this criteria, the condition is true.

- (>=): this one is going to check if the value of the operand on the left side is greater or equal to the one on the right side. If it is true, the condition is true.

Chapter 6: Helping C++ to Make Decisions

There are times when you will need the program to make decisions for you. You are able to set it up to act in a certain way based on the information that the user puts into the computer and what you decide needs to be met for the conditions to be true. The decision making is a bit more advanced inside of this system, but you will find that is pretty easy to learn and will open up a lot of ideas that you are able to work with in the C++ system. Let's take a look at some of the things that you are able to do to help the system to make decisions on its own.

Switch Statements

The first decision that we are going to work with inside of this system are the switch statements. These statements are nice because they are going to allow you to check the equality of your variable against a set of values, or cases. The variable that you are trying to check is going to be compared with each of the cases. A good example of the syntax that you are able to use for this include:

Switch(expression){

    case constant-expression:

    statement(s);

    break; //optional

    case constant-expression:

    statement(s);

    break; //optional

//you can add in as many of these case statements as you would like

Default: //Optional

statement(s);

}

When you are working inside of these statements, there are a few rules that you should keep in mind. First, the expression of the switch statement should be the integral or enumerated class type. In addition, it can also belong to a class that has a conversion function. With C++, there isn't going to be a limit to the amount of case statements that you add into the syntax so you can make them as long or short as you would like. Just remember that you need to have a colon and a value in each of them.

Once the variable finds a value that it is equal to, it is going to keep running until it finds a break statement. The system finds the break statement, the switch is going to stop. Then the control flow will be passed on. You don't need to put in a break statement to the cases. If you end up not having one of these, the control flow will just keep being passed on.

The if statements

One of the most basic things that you are able to do in your programs is create an if statement. These are going to be based on a true and false idea inside the system. If the system says that the input is true with the condition that you set out, then the program is going to run whatever you ask it to. For example, you set it up to have the system as what the answer to 2 + 2 is. If the user puts in the answer as 4, you could have a message come up that says "That is Correct! Good Job!"

Any time that the user puts in an input that ends up being true based on the conditions that you are setting out, you are going to get the statement to show up that you picked out. On the other hand, what is going to happen if your person puts in the wrong answer. If they put the answer as 5 to the question above, it is not going to be right and the system is going to see that the answer is false.

Since the if statement is pretty basic, you are going to find that it is not going to be prepared if the person puts in the wrong answer. At this stage, if they put in any number other than 4 for the example above, the screen is just going to go blank and nothing is going to happen. The next type of statement will go more in depth and show you how to get answers based on what the person puts into the system.

The if else statement

Now as we discussed a bit above, there are some limitations that can come up when you are using the if statement. If the person puts in the wrong answer, the screen is just going to go blank and this can be a pain with the system. Plus, there are times when the user will need to put in a variety of answers, such as when they will put in their age and you want to separate those out. Their age is not necessarily wrong, but if you just want people who are older than 21, you want to make sure that an answer comes up correctly along the way.

A good syntax to use in order to work with the if else statements include:

if(boolean_expresion)

{

    //statement(s) will execute if the boolean expression is true

}

Else

{

// statement(s) will execute if the boolean expression is false

}

You are able to add in as many of these into your statement as you would like. So if you would like to have a program that set apart people in five different age groups, you could set that up based on more of the "else" in your syntax. This makes it easier to add in some other choices.

So let's keep it simple. Let's say that you have 2 +2 on the system. If the person guesses that 4 is the answer, you can set that up in the first part to be the true statement and then the message "That's Right! Good Job!" will come up on the screen. But if the user puts in the answer 5 (or any other answer than 4), you can have a message like "Sorry, that is not the right answer" come up on the screen.

This gives you a lot of freedom when it comes to taking care of what you want to do inside of your code. You are going to be able to add in some different things to the process and you can really expand the code that you are working on.

Another thing that you can keep in mind when working on these, is that you are able to add some if statements and some if else statements inside of each other. This can get a bit complex as a beginner, but with some practice, you will find that it is going to add a lot of power to the whole process and can make it easier to do some of the things that you want within this coding language.

Working with the if statements and the if else statements can make your coding experience so much better. It allows the system to make decisions based on what the user is putting into the system rather than having to be there and do it themselves. Make sure to try out a few of these different types of statements and see how they are going to work within your code and with what you want to do.

Chapter 6: Constants and the various types of Literals

This language is complex, and even though what you have learned above is enough to run some simple functions, there are so many more parts to this language that it would be a crime to not put more in depth knowledge in here to help you transition to the next step.

If you want to be successful with this language, be prepared to spend long hours working hard on it. While it is a good language for beginners as it has multiple levels of difficulties, it is also something that you have to work hard at to make it to the next level. The added effects are more difficult the more you try to learn.

Programming itself is a long and difficult process, but it is definitely worth it, as there are so many professions that you can go into that require the knowledge of C++. From game designing, to working with robots and more. If it involves technology, chances are it involves C++.

So here are some more steps that you can learn, and some more important functions that you need to know to begin to master this language.

Constants and Literals

Constants and literals are an imperative part of learning C++. They refer to data types and variables in those data types. They are constant, and cannot be changed.

They act just like any other variable, other than the fact that they are stagnant and you cannot change them. The integers that you use are known as literal integers. They can have a suffix such as U or L, and they stand for unassigned, and long. These variables are used as uppercase and lowercase and can help your processes along well.

To understand the integer literals, look at some of these examples:

032uu	//illegal: can't repeat your suffix
078	//illegal: 8 isn't considered an octal digit
Ox_Fell	//this one is legal
215	//this one is legal
212	//this one is legal
85	//this one is a decimal
30ul	//this one is an unsigned long
30l	//this one is long
30u	//this one is an unsigned int.
30	//tis one is an int.
Ox4b	//this one is a hexadecimal
0213	//this one is an octal

Floating Point Literals

These are parts of the code that will contain an integer, a decimal point, a fractional part, and an exponent part. These can be shown either through the exponential form or the decimal form.

When you choose to use the decimal point to represent these literals, you need to make sure that you are adding in at least the decimal, although adding in the exponent is good as well. When you are representing through the exponential form, you should include either the fractional part, the integer part, or both of them. The signed exponent that you are using should also be started with either E or e.

Some of the floating point literals that you are able to use in your code writing include:

.e55   //these are illegal because they are missing the fraction or the integer

210f: //these are illegal because they don't have the exponent or the decimal

510E   //these are illegal because they have an incomplete exponent

314159E-5L   //these are legal

3.15159   //these are legal

Boolean Literals

The next type of literal that we can discuss are the Boolean literals. There are two types that you will be able to use inside of your C++ code. Basically the Boolean values are going to be shown as either true or false. If the conditions that you set out are true, the Boolean expression is going to come out as true. On the other hand, if the conditions that you set out are not met, you are going to end up with a condition that is false. All of the answers when they are Boolean will come out either true or false.

Character Literals

When you see a character literal in your code, you will notice that they are closed off with single quotes. These can be simple and use something like 'x' to tell the command or they can be much longer in length as well. These are basic things that you are able to add into your code and can make things much easier to handle.

String Literals

Another type of literal that you are able to work with are the string literals. These are the ones that will be closed off using a double quote. The string is going to contain characters that are like the character literals, including options like universal, escape sequence, and plain characters. You can use the string literal in many ways including to break up one of your lines into two, and separating out things to make it easier to read. Some of the examples of the strings that you can use include:

hello, Mother"

"hello, \

Mother"

"hello, " "M" "other"

Learning how to use some of these different parts inside of the C++ programming language will make a big difference in how well you are able to use this computer language. Have some fun and experiment with using them a bit and you will find that it is easier than ever to get the results that you want!

Conclusion

Thank you again for purchasing this book. I hope that it proved to be informational, but enjoyable. Keep this book as a guide not only for knowledge, but inspiration as well. C++ seems like an intimidating language but the more you practice it in regularity, by days, months, and years, you will achieve complete mastery of this programming language like with anything else in life. I ask you not to fret and be anxious and a problem arise, because there will be many times in which this will happen. There are numerous resources out there for you just waiting to be read of discovered and it is in your best interest to do your due diligence in learning, improving, and enhancing your C++ programming skills to the next level.

Bonus: Brief Hacking History and Overview

Many people have heard the name C++ but really think nothing of it. If you are not very technologically versed then you may think that it is about having a mediocre letter grade, but that is not the case.

Believe it or not, C++ is a hacking language, and while it is not the only one out there, it is one of the more important ones because it is versatile and also easy to use. To learn the most about C++, you have to know more about the reason it came about and that would be hacking.

Hacking

Hacking is not a new concept. For as long as there has been any type of technologies around, there have been people figuring out ways to hack them. Hacking is the manipulations and/or interruptions of any technological stream of data that is being sent from one place to another. This is done with scripts. While you can get pre-packaged scripts online, many people prefer the old fashioned way of writing their own scripts, as is gives them more flexibility to do what the want with the information. Scripts that come already set up into packages have limited mobility and are pretty visible. The goal of a hacker who truly wants to hack is to remain discreet. If you are caught, unless you have permission to be doing what you are doing, you can get in a heap of trouble.

History of Hacking

Hacking began officially in the 1970s when teenagers were banned from using the phone lines because they were trying to make free calls, and figured out how to do so. Phone hacking was the biggest thing, and continued for over a hundred years. Making calls used to be expensive, especially when the phone lines were new, so of course people were trying to find ways to save money, and usually it caught up with them. Such was the case for a man named John Draper. He was arrested for figuring out how to make long distance calls simply by blowing a note into the receiver that prompted it to make a long distance call without an operator. You could then input the number and talk as long as you wish. Genius, but illegal.

He started a revolution though. A group of young teens banded together to create a phone line that hacked the system to help people make free calls. Once this spread like wild fire, Steve Jobs decided to come up with a product that he could market that hacked the phone lines and helped people make free calls by themselves.

Big time computer hacking didn't actually start until the 1980s. However, once it began, it spread like wildfire, and there were a lot of people who thought that it would be a great idea to see what all they could do, and how they could manipulate these computers.

Types of Hacking

There are several different types of hacking out there. And while the media portrays all hackers as bad, they are not. It is not black and white either. While those are the two most popular groups when talking about hacking, there are so many categories in between, that it would not be beneficial to only talk about the two that are most known.

The two main categories that all the sub categories fall between however, are ethical and unethical hacking.

Ethical hacking is hacking that is used only for good purposes. There are a lot of people who have full permissions to hack into a system, and to find all of the bugs of the software or hardware.

Ethical hackers are the ones that are responsible for all of the bug fixes in your phone, apps, tablets, or computers. These people are hired by a company to figure out what is wrong with their systems, and find the best way to fix it. These hackers are an essential part of the hacking community.

If it were not for hackers we would not have the world wide web, urls or HTML. Hacking is an important part if done within the boundaries of ethical hacking.

Unethical hacking, however, is not within the realms of hacking that is legal with current laws. It is hacking for a malicious purpose. People who hack bank mainframes and steal people's credit card and account information and use it to drain accounts are known as unethical hacking.

Unethical hacking is the bane of true hackers existence. These people are the ones that give the good guys a bad name.

Now to go on to the terms for all different types of hackers.

- White Hat Hackers: These are the completely ethical hackers. Every thing that they do is done for good. They go thru a system, and comb it down for any bugs, and build super strong firewalls so that the systems are safe. They create anti-malware software.

- Black Hat Hacking: This is the type of hacking that you have to stay away from. With great power comes great responsibility. The great responsibility to not become prey to the temptation that is black hat hacking. This type of hacking can get you in a lot of trouble, and are immoral. Hacking government files or even other people's privacy can be tempting but will lead to heavy disciplinary actions.

- Grey Hat Hacking: These are the hackers that sometimes do bad things for good reasons. Such as Anonymous. They may hack the firewall of an sensitive information file, but they do so to expose the corruption that is going on behind the firewall. These hackers are often treated like criminals, but in reality, they can be regarded as heroes depending on your perspective.

- Red Hats: These are the bounty hunters of the hacking world. They use their hacking skills to find illegal hackers, such as black hat hackers, or grey hats that are doing bad things that they should not be doing. They then turn them over to the feds, so that the illegal hackers are arrested. There are several other terms for these hackers, but they are not very appropriate, so we shall leave them out.

- Blue Hat Hackers: These are the blue collar workers of the hacking world. They sit in a cubicle and hack away all day to find bugs for Microsoft or other major companies. They clock into a nine to five job that just happens to involve hacking.

These are the main classifications of hackers. There are also elite hackers that spend their entire life becoming the best hackers that the world has seen, and green hat hackers who don't really care about hacking, they just do it for fun. Hacking can be a very useful tool, and even become a profession if you go about it the right way.

Now it is important to note that all of these hackers are going to work in a different way, but they are going to use the same kinds of codes in order to get the information that they want from other computers. A black hat hacker is going to concentrate on getting into the system and getting the information that they need to see success while the white hat hackers are going to work to keep these hackers off the system. While they are working in different ways, they are going to use the same tools and see who will come out on top in the end.

With that said, you need to be careful about what you are doing with your hacking abilities. If you are using them to get onto a system or a network that you aren't allowed to be on, then you could get into a lot of trouble. While some people find these vulnerabilities and tell the company all about them right away, it is still a legal issue if you are on the system when you shouldn't be. The company you mess with could press charges so it is always best to just work within your own network and keep that safe rather than trying to get onto a network you don't belong.

On the other hand, if you are someone who loves to work in the computer world and you want to be able to do this all the time, it may be a good idea to work as a white hat hacker. There are many companies that hold onto private and personal information for their customers, whether it is hospital information, credit card information, or something else. They are always on the lookout for a black hat hacker who may try to get into the system and take this information and a good white hat hacker can always find the work that they need helping these companies out.

Related Titles

[Hacking University: Freshman Edition Essential Beginner's Guide on How to Become an Amateur Hacker](#)

Hacking University: Sophomore Edition. Essential Guide to Take Your Hacking Skills to the Next Level. Hacking Mobile Devices, Tablets, Game Consoles, and Apps
===

Hacking University: Junior Edition. Learn Python Computer Programming From Scratch. Become a Python Zero to Hero. The Ultimate Beginners Guide in Mastering the Python Language

Hacking University: Senior Edition Linux. Optimal Beginner's Guide To Precisely Learn And Conquer The Linux Operating System. A Complete Step By Step Guide In How Linux Command Line Works

Hacking University: Graduation Edition. 4 Manuscripts (Computer, Mobile, Python, & Linux). Hacking Computers, Mobile Devices, Apps, Game Consoles and Learn Python & Linux

Data Analytics: Practical Data Analysis and Statistical Guide to Transform and Evolve Any Business, Leveraging the power of Data Analytics, Data Science, and Predictive Analytics for Beginners

About the Author

Isaac D. Cody is a proud, savvy, and ethical hacker from New York City. Currently, Isaac now works for a mid-size Informational Technology Firm in the heart of NYC. He aspires to work for the United States government as a security hacker, but also loves teaching others about the future of technology. Isaac firmly believes that the future will heavily rely computer "geeks" for both security and the successes of companies and future jobs alike. In his spare time, he loves to analyze and scrutinize everything about the game of basketball.

Made in the USA
Middletown, DE
09 May 2017